YOUR KNOWLEDGE HAS VALUE

- We will publish your bachelor's and master's thesis, essays and papers

- Your own eBook and book - sold worldwide in all relevant shops

- Earn money with each sale

Upload your text at www.GRIN.com and publish for free

Bibliographic information published by the German National Library:

The German National Library lists this publication in the National Bibliography; detailed bibliographic data are available on the Internet at http://dnb.dnb.de .

This book is copyright material and must not be copied, reproduced, transferred, distributed, leased, licensed or publicly performed or used in any way except as specifically permitted in writing by the publishers, as allowed under the terms and conditions under which it was purchased or as strictly permitted by applicable copyright law. Any unauthorized distribution or use of this text may be a direct infringement of the author s and publisher s rights and those responsible may be liable in law accordingly.

Imprint:

Copyright © 2011 GRIN Verlag, Open Publishing GmbH
Print and binding: Books on Demand GmbH, Norderstedt Germany
ISBN: 9783668615106

This book at GRIN:

https://www.grin.com/document/386202

Albert Fernandes

E-Waste. A Great Concern In Eco-Spirituality

GRIN Publishing

GRIN - Your knowledge has value

Since its foundation in 1998, GRIN has specialized in publishing academic texts by students, college teachers and other academics as e-book and printed book. The website www.grin.com is an ideal platform for presenting term papers, final papers, scientific essays, dissertations and specialist books.

Visit us on the internet:

http://www.grin.com/

http://www.facebook.com/grincom

http://www.twitter.com/grin_com

E-WASTE – A GREAT CONCERN IN ECO-SPIRITUALITY

Albert Fernandes

A Seminar Paper Submitted in Partial Fulfilment of the Requirements of the Degree of 'Master of Theology'

2011

Indian Institute of Spirituality, Bangalore, India
St. Peter's Pontifical Institute, Bangalore, India

Contents

1.1 INTRODUCTION 2
1.2 THE TERM ECOLOGY 2
1.3 ELECTRONIC WASTE (E-WASTE) 3
1.3.1 Use and throw away Culture 3
1.3.2 Dangers of E-Waste 4
1.3.3 Its Consequences on Earth 4
1.4 THE SPIRITUALITY OF ECO-REVIVAL - CALL TO BE 'STEWARDS OF GOD'S CREATION' 5
1.4.1 Measures Necessary to Safe-Guard the Earth from E-Waste 6
1.4.2 What can we do? 7
1.5 CONCLUSION 8
BIBLIOGRAPHY 9

1.1 Introduction

Today, Ecology represents a global interest, a question of life and death of humankind and of the whole planetary system. It is the problem of problems and indeed the question that makes relative all other questions and constitutes the new radicalism as well as the actual core of human preoccupations.

Life is one, and human well-being is at its base interwoven with all life on earth and the rhythms of its systems. The suffering of one part means that all creation groans, and rapid global ecological change dramatically displays that suffering.[1]

Today life seems easier with everything just a touch of a button away. We listen to music on swanky mp3 players, iPods, type out important documents on our PCs and laptops, watch movies and television on our brand new plasma or LCD screens, mobile phones, Air Conditions, Refrigerators and other electronic gadgets. However beneath the swanky surface of all this amazing, 'cutting edge' technology lies a dark reality called e-waste.[2] It is very necessary to realize with ecological awareness that being fully human in 21st Century will require being intimate with the earth by caring.[3]

1.2 The Term Ecology

Ecology is evolved from the natural history of the Greeks, particularly Theophrastus, a friend and associate of Aristotle. He first described the interrelationships and between organisms and their non-living environment.[4] The term ecology was coined in 1866 by the German biologist Ernest Haeckel (1834-1919). It derives from two Greek words, '*oikos*', which means 'house' or 'home' and '*logos*' meaning reflection or study.[5] Therefore, ecology means the study of the conditions and relations that make up the habitat of each and every person and indeed, organism in nature. Everything that co-exists pre-exists. And everything that co-exists and

---

[1] Cfr. Catholic Earth Care Australia, 2005: "Remove the Sandals from Your Feet... You are standing on Holy Grounds – An Ecological Vision for Catholic Education in South Australia."– Standing: 22-10-2010. - URL: - http://www.catholicearthcare.org.au/documents/OHG_Web_000.pdf - Electronic Publications.
[2] Cfr. Janjri Jasani: "Pull the Plug on E-waste." In: *The Teenager* 48, No. 10 (October 2010), p. 14.
[3] Cfr. John C. Carmody: "Ecological Consciousness." In: *The New Dictionary of the Cathoic Spirituality* / Michael Downey (ed.). Bangalore: Theological Publications of India, 2003, p. 330.
[4] Cfr. *The New Encyclopedia Britannica* Vol. 6. London: William Benton Publisher, 1974, p. 197; also see Henry Kodikothiyil: *Emerging Trends in Ecological Spirituality* / Unpublished Article. Bangalore: Tejas Vidyapeetha, 2010.
[5] Cfr. Leonardo Boff: *Ecology and Liberation*. New York: Orbis Books, 1992, p. 7.

pre-exists subsists by means of an infinitive web of all inclusive relations. Nothing exists outside relationships.[6] All creatures manifest and possess their own relative autonomy.[7]

Ecology is the study of the interdependence and interaction of living organisms and their environment. Nature, from elementary particles and primordial energy all the way to more complex forms of life, is dynamic; it comprises an intricate network of connections on all sides. All living beings are created and blessed by God.[8]

For Haeckel, a hundred years ago ecology was a branch of biology. It was a subsection of a natural science. Today, for us, it represents a global interest, a question of life and death of humankind and of the whole planetary system. It is the problem of problems and indeed the question that makes relative all other questions and constitutes the new radicalism as well as the actual core of human preoccupations.

1.3 Electronic waste (e-waste)

Electronic waste (e-waste) is a term that is used loosely to refer to obsolete, broken, or irreparable electronic devices like television, computer central processing units (CPUs), computer monitors (flat screen and cathode ray tubes), laptops, printers, scanners and associated wiring and the most commonly used CFl bulbs and mobile phones. E-waste has become a concern in the United States due to the high volumes in which it is generated, the hazardous constitutes it often contains (such as lead, mercury and chromium), and the lack of regulations applicable to its disposal or recycling.[9]

1.3.1 Use and throw away Culture

This new and definitely unwise culture is leading to even more e-waste as we constantly upgrade, update and ultimately abandon one electronic good after another. Recognizing the importance of this throw away culture, companies that manufacture electronic goods now design them to fail or become out-dated sooner, leading consumers to throw them away and replace them faster and the vicious cycle continues. The long and the short of this use and disuse cycle is that we not only have a mounting e-waste problem but that we also waste

---

[6] Cfr. Leonardo Boff: p. 10.
[7] Cfr. K. S. Shrader: *Method in Ecology*. Florida: Cambridge University Press, 1993, p. 4.
[8] Cfr. Mary C. Grey: "Humility." In: *The New SCM Dictionaries of Christian Spirituality* / Philip Sheldrake (ed.). London: SCM Press, 2005, pp. 348-351.
[9] Cfr. Linda Luther: "Managing Electronic Waste: Issues with Exporting E-Waste." In: *CRS Report for Congress*, September 27, 2010; also Cfr. Janjri Jasani: "Pull the Plug on E-waste." In: *The Teenager* 48, No. 10 (October 2010), pp. 14-15.

water, energy and other natural resources in manufacturing newer and 'better' goods faster and faster.[10]

1.3.2 Dangers of E-waste

Under most circumstances, e-waste can legally be disposed of in a municipal solid waste landfill or recycled with few environmental regulatory requirements. This led to encourage recycling which further caused new questions about both e-waste and recycling. With that increase have come new questions about e-waste management. Instead of questions only about the potential impacts associated with e-waste disposal, questions have arisen regarding the potential danger associated with e-waste recycling – particularly when recycling involves the export of e-waste to developing countries where there are few requirements to protect workers of the environment.[11]

Answering questions about both e-waste disposal and recycling involves a host of challenges. Although there may be limited data regarding how e-waste is managed, the consequences of export to countries that manage in improperly are becoming increasingly evident. Various reports and studies (by the mainstream media, environmental organizations, and university researchers) have found primitive waste management practices in India and various countries in Africa and Asia. Operations in Guiyu in the Shantou region of China have gained particular attention. Observed recycling operations involve burning the plastic coverings of materials to extract metals for scrap, openly burning circuit boards to remove solder or soaking them in acid baths to strip them for gold or other metals. Acid baths are then dumped into surface water. Among other impacts to those areas have been elevated blood lead levels in children and soil and water contaminated with heavy metals.[12]

1.3.3 Its Consequences on Earth

It is difficult to determine how much e-waste is exported from the United States to developing countries. It is further difficult to determine how much of the waste that is exported is sent to facilities that will manage it safely as opposed to those that use disassembly and disposal methods that will expose workers to toxic chemicals with little, if any, protection. It is also difficult to determine how much e-waste may be sent to countries that have a limited

---

[10] Cfr. Janjri Jasani: p. 16.
[11] Cfr. Linda Luther: "Managing Electronic Waste: Issues with Exporting E-Waste." 12-10-2010. - Standing: 22-10-2010.- URL:- http://environmental-legislation.blogspot.com/2010/10/managing-electronic-waste-issues-with.html - Electronic Publications.
[12] Cfr. Linda Luther: "Managing Electronic Waste: Issues with Exporting E-Waste." In: *CRS Report for Congress*, September 27, 2010.

regularity framework to protect the local environment – potentially exposing the surrounding communities to resulting contamination. What is becoming easier to note is the impact that e-waste exports are having on less developed nations. With increased exports have come increased media attentions on the improper handling of e-waste in those areas and its resulting impacts.[13]

Various reports have graphically documented health and safety threats to workers and environmental contamination from e-waste recovery practices in developing countries. It is difficult to note all e-waste recycling hubs, but popular destinations for e-waste exported from the United States (and other developed countries) are waste processing operations in Guiyu in the Shantou region of China, Delhi and Bangalore in India, and the Agbogbloshie site near Accra, Ghana. Therefore multiple studies have found out environmental and health effects of uncontrolled waste processing activities. Environmental impacts include contamination of all local environmental media – soil, air, surface water, and ground water. For example it was found out that the primary hazardous recycling operations in Guiyu involve: metal recovery that involves open burning of wires to obtain steel and copper, cathode ray Tube (CRT) cracking to obtain copper-laden yokes, disordering and burning of circuit boards to remove solder and chips, and acid stripping chips for gold; plastic recycling through chipping and melting; and dumping of materials that cannot be further processed (such as CRT glass and burned circuit boards) and residues from recycling operations (such as ashes from open burn operations, spent acid baths, and sludges).[14]

When electronics are not properly disposed of or recycled these toxic materials can be released into the environment through landfill leachate or incinerator ash – both potential pathways to pollution that can negatively affect nearby communities and the health of community members.[15]

1.4 The Spirituality of Eco-Revival - Call to be 'Stewards of God's Creation'[16]

"In the beginning God created the heavens and the earth...God saw all that he had made, and it was very good (Gen 1:1, 31). The scriptures affirm that the *earth is the Lord's and everything in it* (Psalm 26:1). In Gen 1:28, God charges humanity to care for the earth by giving humanity 'dominion' over it. The word 'dominion' is most appropriately translated as

---

[13] Cfr. Linda Luther: "Managing Electronic Waste: Issues with Exporting E-Waste."
[14] Ibid.
[15] Cfr. James F. McKenzie et al. (eds.): *An Introduction to Community Health*. London: Jones and Bartlett Learning, 2008, p. 460.
[16] Cfr. World Council of Churches: *Minutes on Global Warming and Climate Change*, Doc. GEN/PUB, 2008.

'stewardship', [17] since humanity is not the master of the earth but steward to responsibly care for the integrity of creation. God wondrously and lovingly created a world with more than enough resources to sustain generations upon generations of human beings and other living creatures. But humanity is not always faithful in its stewardship. Mindless production and excessive consumption by individuals, corporations and countries have led to continuous desecration of creation, including global warming and other forms of climate change.

Being good stewards leads to a reciprocal relationship between people and the earth.[18] We are dependent on the earth and must take care of it. If we do so, the land and oceans will yield bountiful and sufficient for all. Conversely, if human societies damage the earth, people suffer. Therefore, in this context of contamination of earth due to e-waste we ought to take concrete measures to protect the earth and all its creatures.

1.4.1 Measures Necessary to Safe-Guard the Earth from e-Waste

E-waste collected for recycling may be reused or processed for parts or components. Unlike recyclable products that contain essentially a single component, like plastic bottles or newspaper, electronic devices contain a host of mixed materials that may not be easily separated or extracted. Before the device can be recycled it may go through any of a number of steps, including some or all of the following.

1. Demanufacturing into subassemblies and components – involves a worker manually disassembling a device or component to recover value from working and nonworking components (e.g., video cards, circuit boards, cables, wiring, plastic or metal housings).
2. Depollution – the removal and separation of certain materials to allow them to be handled separately to minimize impacts to human health and the environment (eg., batteries, fluorescent lamps, CRTs, or plastics embedded with brominated flame retardants).
3. Materials Separation – manually separating and preparing material for further processing. At the stage, materials that have already been disassembled would be sorted into material categories.
4. Mechanical Processing of Similar Materials – generally involves processing compatible plastic rains, metals, or CRT glass to generate market-grade commodities.
5. Mechanical processing of mixed materials – generally involves processing whole units, after depollution, followed by a series of separation technologies.

---

[17] Cfr. Sallie McFague: *The Body of God*. Minneapolis: Fortress Press, 1993, p. 91.
[18] Cfr. K. S. Shrader: *Method in Ecology*. Florida: Cambridge University Press, 1993, pp. 170-171.

6. Metal refining / smelting – after being sorted into components or into shredded streams, metals can be sent to refiners or smelters. At this stage, thermal and chemical management processes are used to extract metals of many types. [19]

Many of the processes described above must be done by hand and can be labour intensive. This can be a costly operation.

1.4.2 What can we do?

Thankfully, it's not all darkness and gloom and there's a lot we can do to sort out this problem of e-waste. "Over thirty electronics recycling companies had signed a pledge – initiated by the Basel Action Network, Silicon Valley Toxics Coalition, and the other NGOs that make up the Computer TakeBack Campaign – agreeing not to export hazardous e-waste to poorer countries."[20] STOP gravitating towards this throw-away culture. Don't throw away your old mobile phone just because a newer model has come out with a marginally larger screen. If you're updating your computer just buy a new memory card, hard drive or software instead of chucking the whole deal and starting with all new equipment. If your fridge breaks down go to your repairman and not an appliances store and when printer cartridges run dry, just refill them instead of retiring them. Giving away or selling used electronics are great ways to extend their use and keep them out of landfills.[21]

One should not entertain anyone to throw away the waste anywhere. "Disposal and recycling of computer waste in the country has become a serious problem since the methods of disposal are very rudimentary and pose grave environmental and health hazards."[22] Today, India remains a favourite dumping ground for plastic wastes, mostly from northern nations such as the United States, Canada, Denmark, Germany, the United Kingdom, the Netherlands, Japan, and France. According to the Indian Government, at least 59,000 tons and 61,000 tons of plastic were imported in 1999 and 2000, respectively. Many activities in India and other parts of South Asia are hopeful and see the possibility for reversing the tide of environmental injustice.[23] Therefore, we need to use electronic goods very reasonably.

---

[19] Cfr. Linda Luther: "Managing Electronic Waste: Issues with Exporting E-Waste."
[20] Elizabeth Grossman: *High Tech Trash – Digital Devices, Hidden Toxics, and Human Health.* Washington: Island Press, 2006, p. 201.
[21] Cfr. Janjri Jasani: "Pull the Plug on E-waste." In: *The Teenager* 48, No. 10 (October 2010), p. 16.
[22] David Naguib Pellow: *Resisting Global Toxics – Transnational Movements for Environmental Justice.* Cambridge: MIT Press, 2007, p. 199.
[23] Cfr. David Naguib Pellow: *Resisting Global Toxics – Transnational Movements for Environmental Justice*, p. 142.

Become a responsible consumer. What does this mean? Well, it just means buying your electronic goods from those companies that have a good track record when it comes to e-waste, whose products have fewer toxics and more recyclable parts when compared to their competitors. Greenpeace recently conducted a study and scored some of the biggest names in electronics on an eco-e-waste score card.[24] E-waste is a very important social problem and we need to have scientific management of e-waste to prevent pollution and protect people's lives.[25]

Reduce the amount of unnecessary packaging and adopt practices that reduce waste toxicity. Consider reusable products. Maintain and repair durable products. Reuse bags, containers and other items. Borrow, rent, or share items used infrequently. Sell or donate goods instead of throwing them out. Choose recyclable products. And most of all educate others on source reduction and recycling practices. Make your preferences known to manufacturers, merchants, and community leaders. Above all be creative – find new ways to reduce waste quality and toxicity.[26]

1.5 Conclusion

E-waste not only contaminates the developed countries but even the developing countries like India, China and Africa where most of the e-waste is intentionally dumped. To fight against such injustice done towards humanity and environment, every human should practice "life in all its fullness" (John 10:10) in the face of a modern materialism that has now been globalized. The central committee of the World Council of Churches, meeting in Geneva, Switzerland, 13-20 February 2008 urgently calls the churches:

- To strengthen their moral stand in relationship to global warming and climate change, recalling its adverse effects on poor and vulnerable communities in various parts of the world.
- For a profound change in the relationship towards nature, economic policies, consumption, production and technological patterns.

We need to take care of the creation of God where humans have an obligatory duty to safeguard other species. Our greed for progress and development should not destroy the other species on earth. That is the duty of every human being 'to preserve what is GOOD.'

---

[24] Cfr. Janjri Jasani, p. 16.
[25] Cfr. Elizabeth Grossman: *High Tech Trash – Digital Devices, Hidden Toxics, and Human Health*, p. 197.
[26] Cfr. James F. McKenzie et al. (ed): *An Introduction to Community Health*. London: Jones and Bartlett Learning, 2008, p. 460, p. 459.

BIBLIOGRAPHY

CATHOLIC EARTH CARE AUSTRALIA, 2005: "Remove the Sandals from Your Feet... You are standing on Holy Grounds – An Ecological Vision for Catholic Education in South Australia."– Standing: 22-10-2010. - URL: - http://www.catholicearthcare.org.au/documents/OHG_Web_000.pdf - Electronic Publications.

PELLOW, David Naguib: *Resisting Global Toxics – Transnational Movements for Environmental Justice.* Cambridge: MIT Press, 2007, p. 199.

GROSSMAN, Elizabeth: *High Tech Trash – Digital Devices, Hidden Toxics, and Human Health.* Washington: Island Press, 2006, p. 201.

MCKENZIE, James F. et al. (ed): *An Introduction to Community Health.* London: Jones and Bartlett Learning, 2008, p. 460, p. 459.

JASANI, Janjri: "Pull the Plug on E-waste." In: *The Teenager* 48, No. 10 (October 2010), p. 14.

CARMODY, John C.: "Ecological Consciousness." In: *The New Dictionary of the Cathoic Spirituality* / Michael Downey (ed.). Bangalore: Theological Publications of India, 2003, p. 330.

SHRADER, K. S.: *Method in Ecology.* Florida: Cambridge University Press, 1993, p. 4.

BOFF, Leonardo: *Ecology and Liberation.* New York: Orbis Books, 1992, p. 7.

LUTHER, Linda: "Managing Electronic Waste: Issues with Exporting E-Waste." 12-10-2010. - Standing: 22-10-2010.- URL:- http://environmental-legislation.blogspot.com/2010/10/managing-electronic-waste-issues-with.html - Electronic Publications.

LUTHER, Linda: "Managing Electronic Waste: Issues with Exporting E-Waste." In: *CRS Report for Congress*, September 27, 2010.

GREY, Mary C.: "Humility." In: *The New SCM Dictionaries of Christian Spirituality* / Philip Sheldrake (ed.). London: SCM Press, 2005, pp. 348-351.

MCFAGUE, Sallie: *The Body of God.* Minneapolis: Fortress Press, 1993, p. 91.

THE NEW ENCYCLOPEDIA BRITANNICA Vol. 6. London: William Benton Publisher, 1974, p. 197; also see Henry Kodikothiyil: *Emerging Trends in Ecological Spirituality* / Unpublished Article. Bangalore: Tejas Vidyapeetha, 2010.

WORLD COUNCIL OF CHURCHES: *Minutes on Global Warming and Climate Change*, Doc. GEN/PUB, 2008.

YOUR KNOWLEDGE HAS VALUE

- We will publish your bachelor's and
  master's thesis, essays and papers

- Your own eBook and book -
  sold worldwide in all relevant shops

- Earn money with each sale

Upload your text at www.GRIN.com
and publish for free